Little Lights

Tanya Bass

BookLeaf
Publishing

India | USA | UK

Presentation by *BookLeaf Publishing*

Web: www.bookleafpub.com

E-mail: info@bookleafpub.com

ISBN: 978-93-5744-350-0

First edition 2022

DEDICATION

Hi Dad

I wrote this one for you. Thank you for being there, I hope you can hear us read them. Keep shining for us. RIP.

ACKNOWLEDGEMENT

I would like to thank my Mother and Father: Kay and Nigel, for supporting me with my love for poetry. I would also like to thank my sister, Alissa, for guiding me.

PREFACE

Writing has always been more of a hobby for me, however at the age of 16, I really started becoming more interested in poetry. This book holds a collection of poems written some in the last year, most within the last month, many of which I hold very closely to my heart.

To Dad

Thank you
For being an amazing Dad
My Dad
For helping me mend my mistakes
For the comfort
     Advice
For cheering me up on a bad day;
For encouraging us to believe
That we are, and can be strong,
That we are defiant.

And with you,
In a busy crowd, or even together in silence
You lift me up
To stand on the shoulders of a giant.

Superpowers

I wish I had superpowers
    Like telepathy, that would be cool.
I wouldn't have had to speak out at school,
Hear my voice break saying
"When I was in hospital..."
I'd just tell them in their heads.
No need for tears
Or trembling voices
I'd sit undisturbed, happy instead.

I'd love to have superpowers
   Like flying! Or running really fast
I'd get to appointments so quick, I would never miss class
Or run out of energy
Get tired
Because I hadn't taken my meds.
Not yawning, not drowsy
Not longing for my bed.

Superpowers would be awesome! I know
Like turning back time.
I would disguise myself, find my parents
Tell them everything would be fine.
I'd whisper in my younger-self's ear

To "make the most of life", as I slept in bed.
Maybe then I'd be reassured,
Erase the dreams full of dread.

Although, I reckon
I do have a superpower.
Some have heard
That I'm pretty good at listening,
No actions, not saying a word.
I'm there, present
And I hear your concerns,
all your stories
    Emotions running wild.

And then, maybe you'll feel better
I get it
        I get you: grown up and child

You and I, we are not merely those whom time
forgot.
How do I know?
Because WE are super, I mean it,
Because together, we've been through a lot.

When the World's Not Watching

When the world's not watching
I'd sing out loud as I walk to the beat,
Do a little dance
...or a big one,
Kick a can and not pick it up
As I walk along the street.

Maybe I'd turn on the TV, then walk out the
room,
Leave the washing up, and just
Buy new dishes;
Eat a ready meal for two.

I might drive over the speed limit
...what limit?
I'd turn corners in 3rd gear,
Speak lazily, like the kids from the block,
That's cool innit...
Cycle with no hands, no fear.

When the world's not watching
Maybe I'd feel calmer, and free
My blood pressure would go down, maybe
I could relax
Admit that I don't like tea,
And I would maybe be happy being me.

Hospital Patience

From my spot
In the hospital coffee shop
I see time freeze
In a clinical bubble
Of crutches and drips,
Where older faces predominate at tables
People in gowns
Wearing tatty wrist labels
Looking up at the clinic list,
Holding their tea
Taking small sips.

To my left: the reception
Where staff stand stock still
With square faces,
Right now, remaining silent,
Unhelpfully stating,
"Not currently working,
"Please sign in at other places".

And us, still sitting here
In the simple coffee shop
Safe of the ground
Oblivious to the pain
Of those lying above,

Except maybe for loved ones,
Holding their mugs with strong grasps
Wondering
Dreading
How long their patience could last.

Graduate

Standing together
Heads held high
We made it! Yes..you
And me,
Hearts uplifted as our caps soar
Reaching the sky.
All of you more than colleagues
And peers.
Connected,
We are a force
Not merely bound by our careers.

So we wear our caps with pride,
Exchange our scrubs for our best dresses,
Two years of highs
Maybe a few lows..
But these moments have made us… well.. us.

We are Braver, Stronger, Wiser,

And it shows.

Hello Dear

I miss you, Dad.
Your laugh, your hugs,
All the adventures we were still to have.
Your non-presence stands out,
Dinner conversations lack
the deeper tone
of your voice.
I want you back
I need you here
I miss you, Dad.
And to hear those words
one more time.
"Hello dear".

Not Well

I'd love to say, "I'm fine what about you?"
And mean it,
To keep living in the "now".
I want to be able to relax each day
Knowing I've done my best
And that I deserve a rest.
I want to be truly "f-i-n-e"
But I don't know how.

I'd love to hear each sentence as you say it
And not analyse each word
To hear the judgement between the lines
And my chest punching threats of crying.
I want to be able to stop
Putting obscure
Amounts of energy into smiling,
To feel like my face isn't lying.

In a world where it's bad to feel fear
Where it's shameful to shed tears,
I had always hoped for better.
Is that it?
As good as it gets?
I really hope it gets better from here.

Tumour

A part of me
For so many years.
Growing slowly, making space
Pushing vessels out of place;
Gradually breaking me apart
From inside out.
All the while
Slowing my heart,
Draining my energy,
Stunting me growth.
Needless to say
My companion was killing me,

It made itself known
Loud
Proud
So superior
Not even my thoughts were allowed.
But then one day
Gone
Clean cut - out of the race.
And for a while,

Relief.

I felt I could live again, b r e a t h e ... .
.

But even now, strangely
A sense of something missing.

Nothing to fill the now empty space.

Pallium

If you lived across the galaxy and beyond the
stars,
I'd jump to Jupiter, to Venus, to Mars;
Fly rocket from earth to get lightyears away,
And get closer to you, even just for a day.

If you were trapped on an island: just trees and
sand,
I'd tie a rope to the continent, drag you closer to
land
Or give you a boat, and get the breeze blowing;
Light stars in the clear night, so you know where
you're going.

If you told me you ad cancer, had 1 more year,
I'd stay close to you, I'd hide my tears
Because I know you're strong, always up for a
fight,
You say, "look, the finish line's just in sight"...

And if I found out it was our last day together
I'd freeze time to stay together forever
Nothing else would matter just us against the
world
You'd get to live the best and fullest life you
deserved.

Yet, I knew one day, I'd find you gone
That hole in my heart won't heal for so long.
But there's no point wondering what, why, how...
Because I was blessed with the time we shared
together
And my memory of you right now.

Defiance

My life: A Quest
And I am worthy
I am strong.
Tell it to myself daily,
With no doubt,
I am liked
I am loved
I belong,
And I know I can do anything
Anything.
I am mighty
And this right here
Is my heart-song .

My bravery shines with Tumour-Defiance,
And I shall not
Be
Silenced.

My journey continues
I move forward.
Head held high, I can touch the stars
And I stand tall amongst a crowd of giants.

To The Garden

Through our kitchen window
 I see your world
  Of trees
   Birds
    Green, green grass
     Brown, crispy leaves
Orange, yellow, gold and brass

An unevenly laid lawn
So perfectly rolled out;
Grandad's tree at the end
With red leaves
Bold, dark bark,
Stands outright and proud;
The blue sky, lined with
Apples and pears
Each tree growing for years
And years.

All the care you gave it,
And it loved you so much too,
In the weeks before your passing
Your crop failed to grow
As if somehow
The garden knew

And felt
Something we didn't know.

You lived amongst them then,
Even more so now,
How you still keep it all growing
We'll never know how.

From rolling pebbles,
Falling leaves,
Dropping conkers,
To sprouting saplings
And pushing up daisies,
Your love for the garden
Continues to amaze me.

Trees and plants stand tall in your honour
And I hope I can keep it going
Just as I know you'll help me still
To keep the plants growing.

Being Adult

I wake on hearing the rude cry
Of my alarm on my mobile phone.
I slowly peep open my eyes
And let out a frustrated moan.
What felt like 5 minutes was apparently
A 7.5 hour sleep.
No time to have a 10 minute long nap,
Or stay in bed and weep.
I make and eat breakfast in 15 minutes
Go upstairs for teeth to brush
I don't do my hair, it's work, who cares?
Leave the house in a massive rush.

Urgh I hate this malarkey of adult life
It's really so berserk
How I miss my years in education
Now living for my work.

Ears

Please listen
All I ask, right now
Is to be held, perhaps it may lift a burden.
That gift of listening
It's what I long for
It's what I'm missing

So please, just this once,
Maybe withhold your advice
And well-meaning words
I can't take them

Not yet.

I yearn for a shoulder to lean on.
When I open up
Please lend me your ears
For this moment
All I ask you to give
Is a tissue for my tears.

Twin

I am not you
And you are not me
Our genetic similarities
May be hard to see,
But I feel them... maybe you do
Too.
Like the overwhelming happiness
At your successes;
The sadness when you feel blue;
And the guilt
When I can't share my joy with you.
Yes, it's tiring
Feeling the emotions of two.
But hear me.

It's worth every smile and tear
From big events to little things,
What we share year on year.
I hear your voice every day,
And any distance between us
Pulls tighter on my heart strings,
So I value every moment
Together
Because the separation stings,

Yet... somehow
Knowing that you're happy
And healthy
That warms me to the core
And I know you'll be just as
AMAZING
As you are here,
I couldn't ask for anything more.

Cat

Oh you big fat feline
With large blue eyes.
How you think you're hiding,
Cleverly disguised
Amongst the tall green grass
No a cat in sight…
Yet, you fail to realise,
Your coat is white.

You silly old cat
Always aiming so high
Your dreams live amongst
Those juicy birds in the sky.
On your perch, there's nothing
Out of reach, or "too distant"
You always mean to crash to the floor
Dash off in an instant.

Sir Meowsworthy of the House
Far too royal for cat nibble
When I prepare food for human,
You start to dribble.
Roast chicken so juicy
"For me? Oh so good of her"
later finding my dinner
Half eaten on the counter.

This big old fluffball,
He's not even mine
He belongs to the neighbours
They must think its fine
He spends hours on our sofa
Curls up on our bed
Why bother getting out own?
He's adopted us instead.

That's my cake

A slice of cake please
Always always chocolate
No to icing
Unless its frosting
But don't give me a lot.

Make sure there's plenty of filling
The correct cake to cream
Proportion
And big enough to give my friend and me
2 decent-sized portions

Top it off with sprinkles
Now that looks really nice
But I just have to say,
That I've had a pretty tough day…

So I want the bigger slice!

Mum

My superhero
Lives in a bungalow
With a huge garden, neat flower beds
With a vegetable patch growing
Beans, cabbages, tomatoes.

Washes dishes at the speed of light
With the clap of a hand
Can stop a fight
And no bully would dare confront
Her power and might
She is strong
She is Just
Puts her family first without a fuss.

Barely five foot small
She stands so tall,
But never overshadows me.
She helps me to grow,
Shine
And helps me to see
A greater future,
Believes in the best of me.

Takeaway

Come Saturday night
I eagerly wait,
I anticipate
To hear you say,
"I think I'd like a takeaway".
Then, I fly to the drawer
Of unexplored cuisine
And old reliables.
We scan our options,
All seem so palatable.

Maybe this time
We'll have an Indian,
No wait! Thai, or Sushi,
Or Chinese!
No one else we have to please
With our own choice.
We could have pizza
Or fish and chips,
The scrolling through of menu,
As I unconsciously
Lick my lips.

The best part of a takeaway
Though
Is not merely the type of food.
No.
It's the debate of which restaurant,
Browsing a menu
And spending more time with you.
My time passes so quickly
When waiting for the doorbell to ring,
That I forget we've ordered food.

So thank you,
For splitting the bill with me,
As I'll gladly
Share my time with you.

Milky

I still sleep with my childhood teddy
I got him when I was three
Always protects me from nightmares
And welcomes happy dreams.

He's meant to be a polar bear
With soft, white, fluffy fur
But after 22 years of love
He's stained with a little dirt.

When I wake in the night time
And he's not tucked in my arms
I scramble in the bed sheets to find him
So he can keep me safe and warm.

So what? I have a teddy bear.
Why should I be ashamed?
I know he'll never leave me,
And Milky is his name.

Grow Up

6
I want to be a grown-up
Then I can do what I like.
I could eat snack all day
Go out with my friends on my bike.
10
I can't wait to be an adult
I could speak what I think, and vote
Roll my eyes and not get told off
When I hear the bullies gloat.
15
Ugh, I can't wait to be 18,
Then I can drive a car,
Go on nights out with my friends,
Drink alcohol at a bar.
19
It's great being adult,
Others treat me with respect,
And my parents still remind me
What to do when I forget.
25
Things seem a lot harder now
I have to find my own way
No more pocket money, I must save up
Now that I get my own pay.

Can I wish those years back, please?
When I had my whole future planned.
When tomorrow was always certain.
When Dad was here to hold my hand.

I'd rather not look ahead anymore,
As I'm scared of what is coming.
No time to stop and take a breath,
As time just keeps on running.

Poet

How do I write a poem?
Do I stick with regular rhymes
Creating a constant rhythm
Rhyming alternate lines?
Or do I branch out a bit
Explore the world
Of spoken word
And phrasing.
Does it really matter what it looks like in the
end?
Does it create the shape of an object?
Does it really have to be "amazing?"

I think a poem should be
What you want it to..
I mean, I like mine to rhyme, although where I
place this,
Often differs.
My topics range from
Heart-felt to funny,
And their contents are far from the sum of me.
I write from my heart,
My brain,
My fingers,
Whatever topic comes to me.
They mean a lot, my poetry.